CW00868359

"Now faith is the substance of things hoped for, the evidence of things not seen.
For by it the elders obtained a good report.
But without faith it is impossible to please Him: for he that cometh to God must believe that He is and that He is a rewarder of them that diligently seek Him."

Hebrews 11:1-2,6

The writer-illustrator is a grandmother who was elated when her then five-year old grandson – who adores reading - declared his belief in God to his mother.

An experienced classroom teacher with over forty years in Africa, France and England, she was judged VERY GOOD by Ofsted inspectors in October 2003.

She enjoys creating different types of teaching and learning resources: activity sheets, quizzes, board and card games and even jig-saw puzzles.

She taught herself to play the keyboard and loves composing inspirational songs.

To begin with, God created heaven and earth.
The earth had no shape and there was nothing in it.
God's Spirit moved over the waters

And God said: Light appear! and there was light.

The light was very good.
God divided the light from the darkness.

And God called the light Day, and the darkness He called Night. And the evening and the morning were the first day.

1st

And God said:

Let the waters break up into two halves!

God made some space to separate the waters: there was water above and water below.

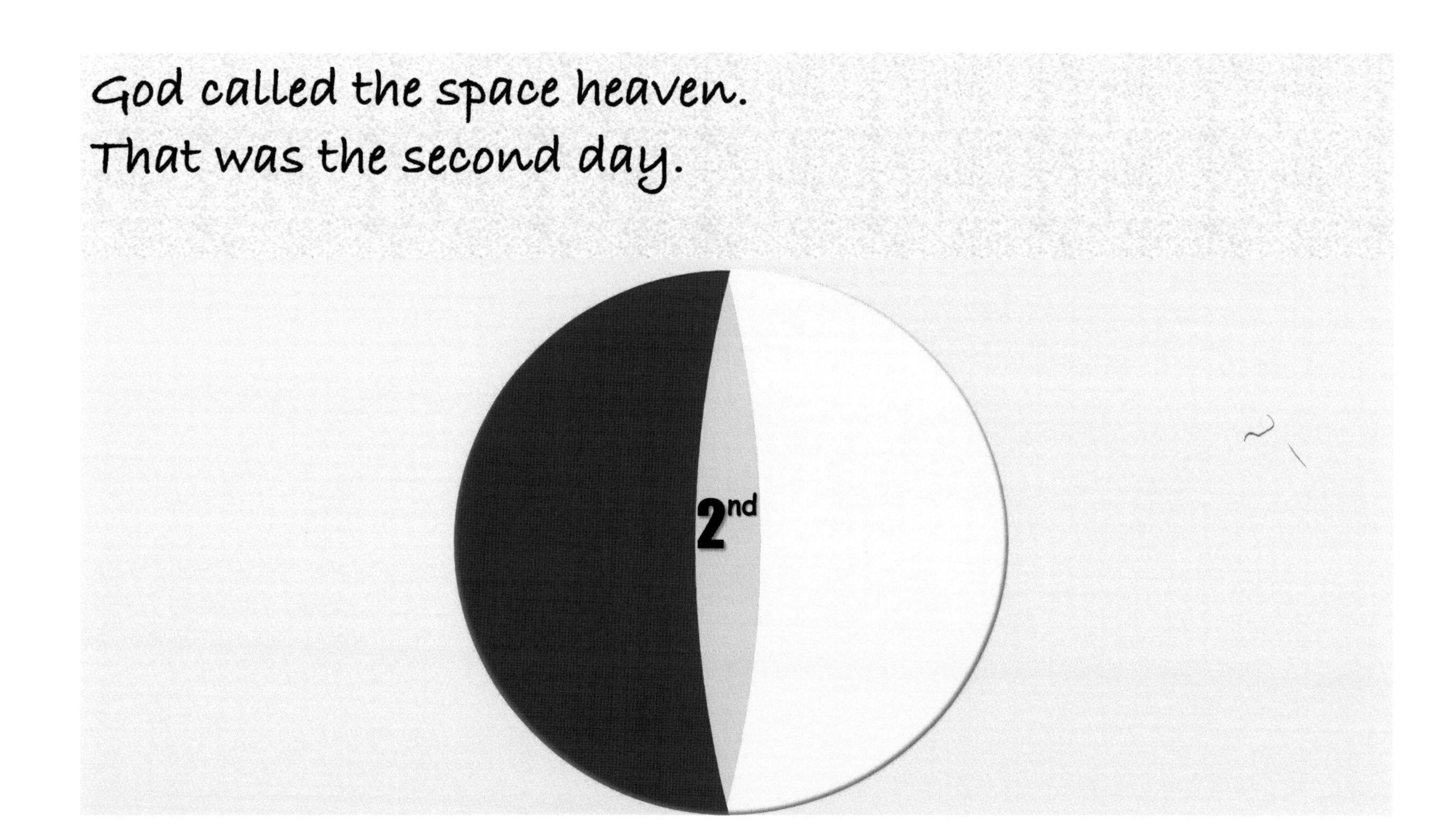
God called the space heaven.
That was the second day.
2nd

God said:

Waters below – gather together
and dry land appear!

So it did.

God called the dry land Earth.
He called the gathered water Sea.

God said:

Earth: grow grass, vegetables, and fruits.

Earth obeyed.

The earth made grass grow.
There were plants and there were fruits on trees.

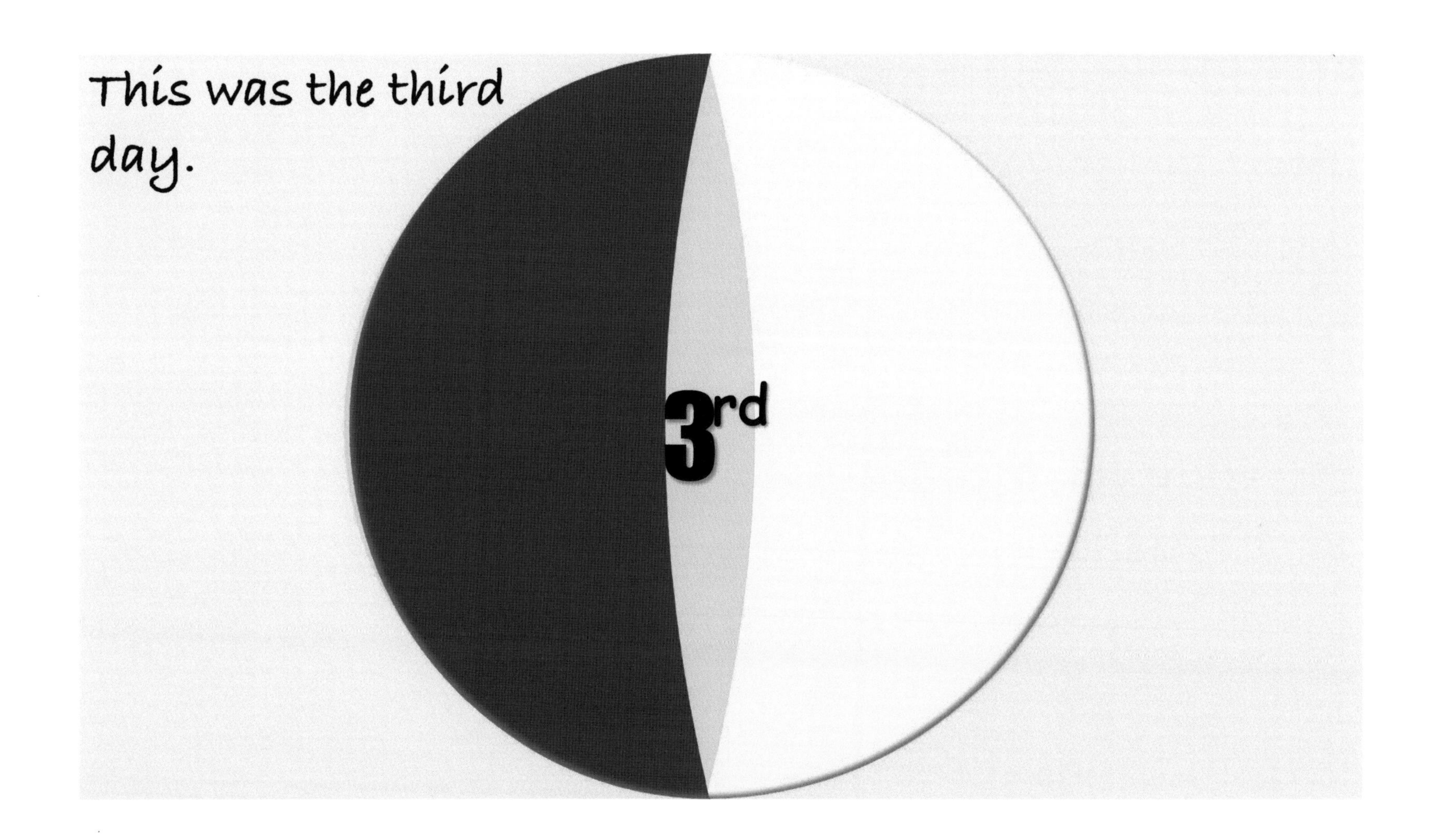
This was the third day.
3rd

AUTUMN
WINTER
SPRING
SUMMER
God commanded lights from heaven: to separate day from night.
The earth has seasons, weeks, months and years.

And God made two great lights:
the bigger, sun, for the day; and the
smaller, moon, for the night.
He also made stars.

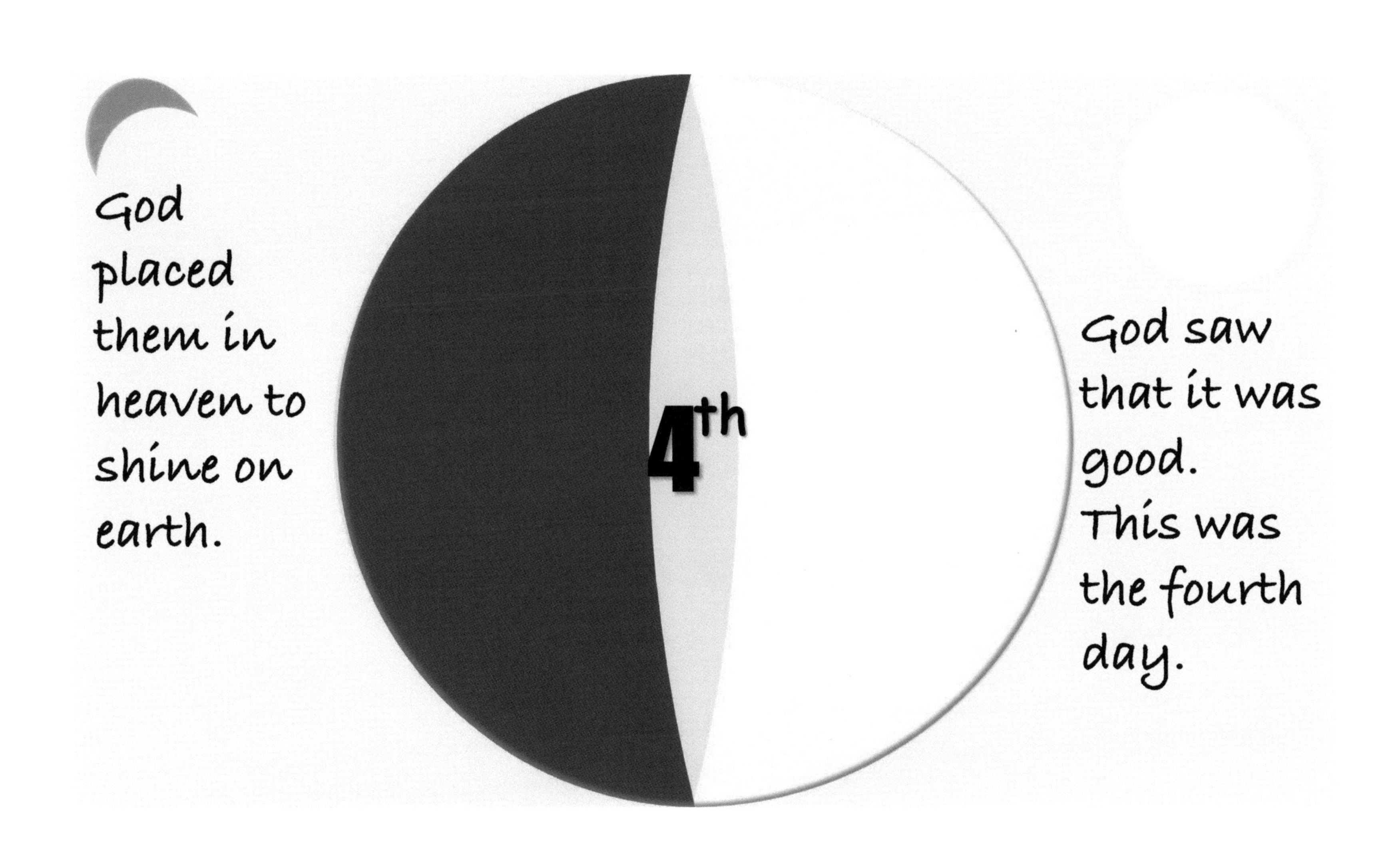
God
placed
them in
heaven to
shine on
earth.
4th
God saw
that it was
good.
This was
the fourth
day.

God said:

Waters, bring forth lots of moving creatures.
Let birds fly in the air!

God created huge whales, and every moving creature.
Land and sea creatures are created to have babies like themsleves.
God saw that it was good.

God blessed them, saying:

Have lots of babies like you and fill up the earth!

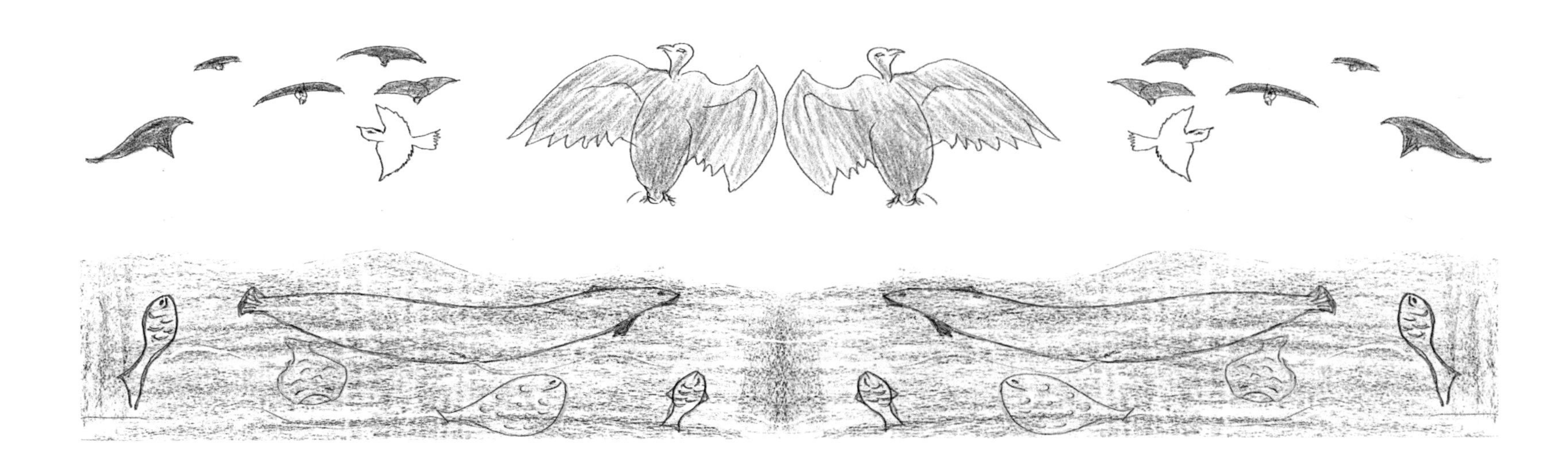

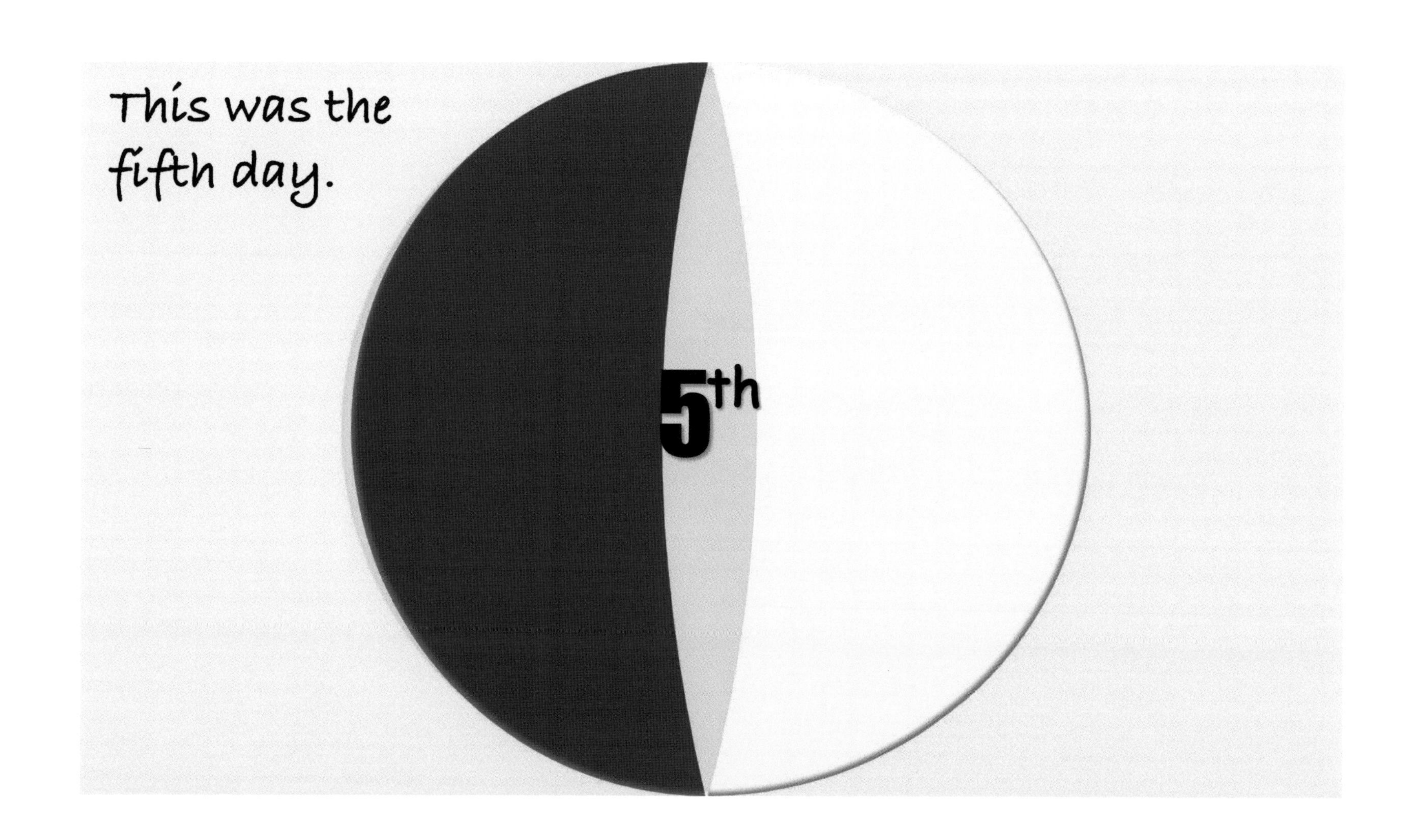
This was the fifth day.
5th

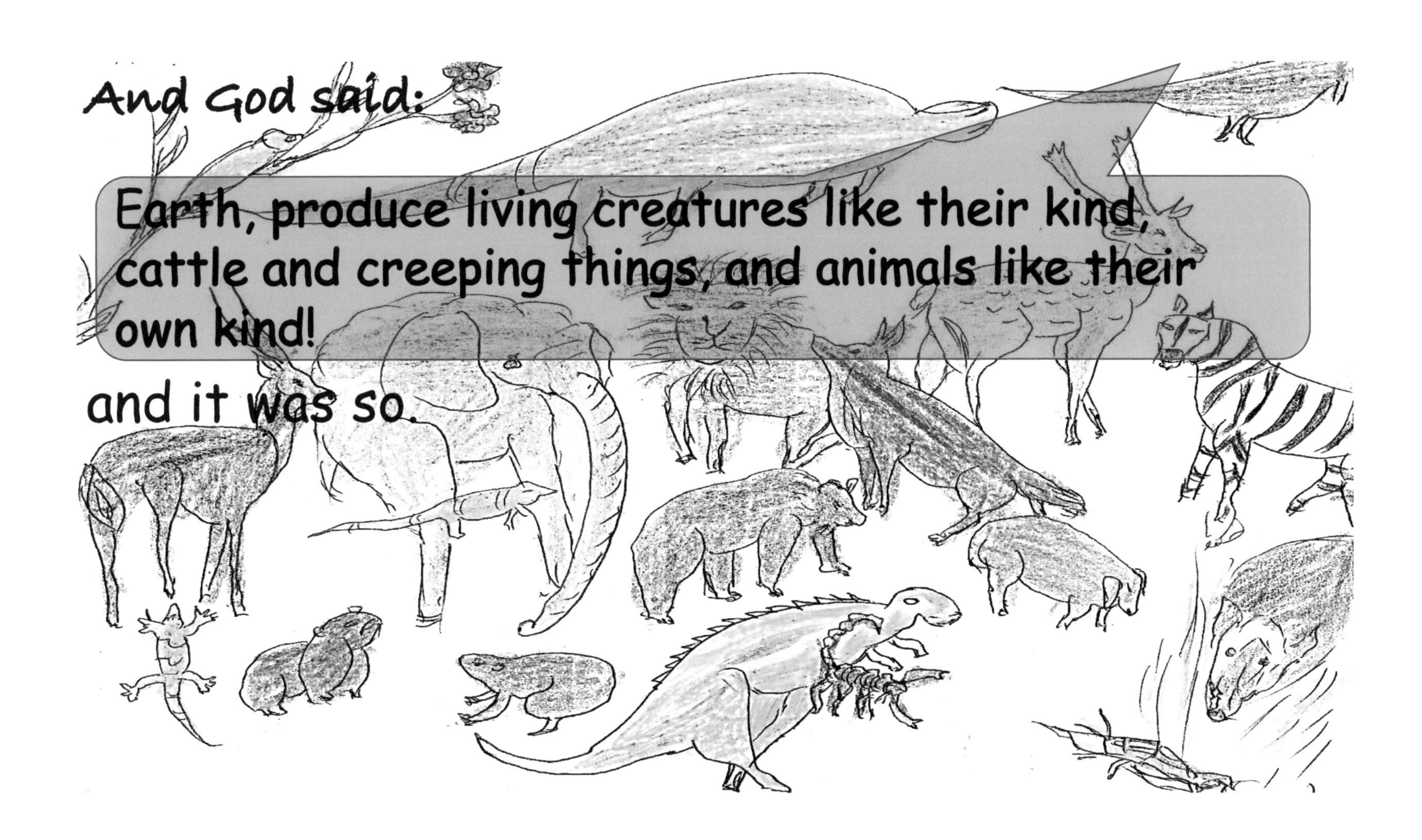
And God said:
Earth, produce living creatures like their kind, cattle and creeping things, and animals like their own kind!
and it was so.

God created animals and birds and creeping things and water creatures all like themselves to reproduce.

And God said:

We will make human beings in our image.
They shall take care of and control all the animals and birds and fishes.

God created man in His own image: male and female.

God blessed Adam and Eve and said to them:

Have children and fill the earth.
Be in charge of all the animals, birds and fishes.

God said:

You may eat all the fruits and vegetables.

I have also given the vegetation for food to all the animals and birds.

God saw everything that
He made was very good
6th
This was the sixth day.

God completed creating heaven and earth and everything in them.
On the seventh day, He rested from all of His work of creating.
God blessed the seventh day because He rested on that day.

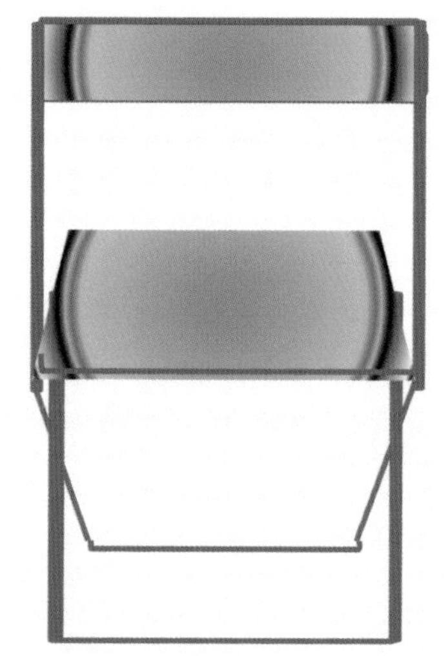

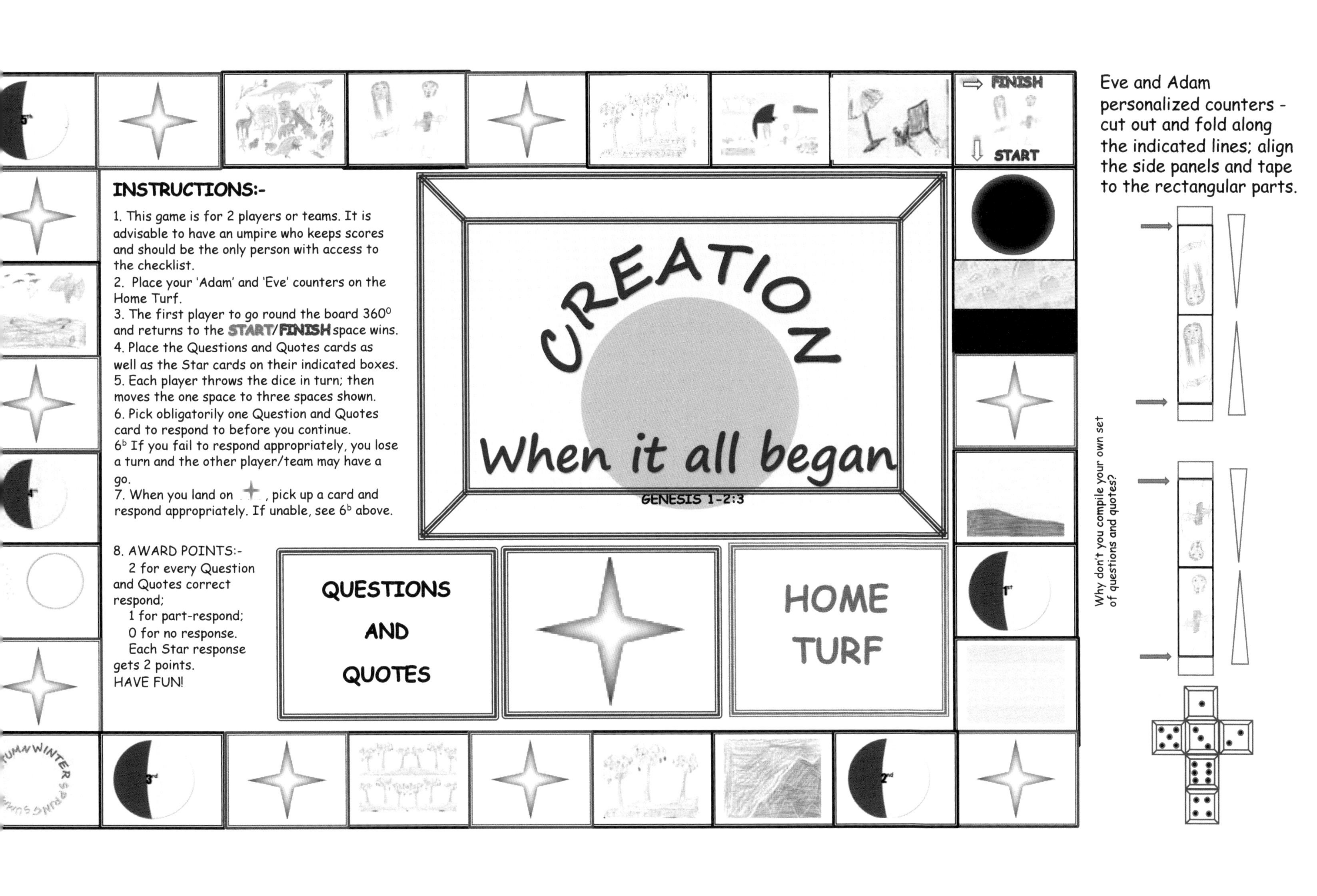
FINISH
START
INSTRUCTIONS:-
1. This game is for 2 players or teams. It is advisable to have an umpire who keeps scores and should be the only person with access to the checklist.
2. Place your 'Adam' and 'Eve' counters on the Home Turf.
3. The first player to go round the board 360⁰ and returns to the START/FINISH space wins.
4. Place the Questions and Quotes cards as well as the Star cards on their indicated boxes.
5. Each player throws the dice in turn; then moves the one space to three spaces shown.
6. Pick obligatorily one Question and Quotes card to respond to before you continue.
6b If you fail to respond appropriately, you lose a turn and the other player/team may have a go.
7. When you land on ✦, pick up a card and respond appropriately. If unable, see 6b above.
8. AWARD POINTS:-
2 for every Question and Quotes correct respond;
1 for part-respond;
0 for no response.
Each Star response gets 2 points.
HAVE FUN!
CREATION
When it all began
GENESIS 1-2:3
QUESTIONS AND QUOTES
HOME TURF
Eve and Adam personalized counters - cut out and fold along the indicated lines; align the side panels and tape to the rectangular parts.
Why don't you compile your own set of questions and quotes?
5th
4th
3rd
2nd
1st
AUTUMN WINTER SPRING SUMMER